What are your life's dreams and desires?

What wisdom would you like to pass on to others?

How could you help to minimize the financial, legal, and emotional difficulties your family and friends may face after your death?

This journal is a place to ask yourself these and many other questions about your life and death. It is an opportunity to prepare for your passing and a place to say good-bye to those you leave behind. It is a way for you to make your mark in history. It is a celebration of you!

REMEMBERING ME

A JOURNAL FOR YOU AND YOUR LOVED ONES

by Danielle Light

Mt. Shasta Publications
Mt. Shasta, California

**Published by MT. SHASTA PUBLICATIONS
P.O. Box 436, Mt. Shasta, California 96067**

Printed by Naturegraph, Happy Camp, California, U.S.A.

ISBN   0-9616478-0-9

Library of Congress Cataloging in Publication Data

Light, Danielle, 1957-
     Remembering Me

1. Life	2. Death		I. Title
BD435.L47	1986	155.9′7	86-5114

All of us have lived a life
worth sharing.
All of us are worth remembering.

D. Light

In Memory Of

Edith Fischel
My grandmother, who showed me the great importance of preparing for death.

Eric B. Clem
My friend, who taught me that there is no such thing as "too young to die."

Garry Bland
My father, whose love is never ending.

Preface

There is a story about a man caught in a flood. A boat comes along to save him but he says, *"No, go away. God will save me."* As the water rises higher, another boat comes along to save him, and to the rescuers he says as before, *"Go away, I believe in God and He will save me."* The water continues to rise around the man, and he is drowning. In the nick of time a helicopter throws down a ladder for him, but he yells out, *"Only God can save me,"* and he drowns. Later, after arriving in Heaven, he says to God, *"I always loved You and believed in you, so why did You let me drown?"*

God then replies, *"What did you want? I sent you two boats and a helicopter!"*

Thinking about my own life, I imagined going to heaven and asking God, *"Why didn't you help me do something with my life?"*

And He replies, *"Well, I gave you about thirty-seven-hundred really good ideas!"*

This book is one of those ideas; one which I know is too important to let pass by. Too important because it is an expression of you. It is a time for self appreciation and acceptance; a time of thoughtfulness and caring. It is your book and with it you are adding to the reservoir of love in the world.

May this book become something very meaningful to you. May you be forever grateful for life and live in daily celebration of it. May all beings be happy.

love,

VII

Acknowledgements

I am very grateful for all the people who have enhanced my life by offering me their love and support. These people know who they are. Some of them have made particular contributions to this book. I would like you to know who they are. Thank you Rachel Bagby, kk Chardin, Delores Clem, Bill Colclough, Jan Davis, Mitch Earle, Ken Goodrich, Suren Holbek, Inja Ink, Nancy & Paul Jameson, Jack Kornfield, William Lapaz, Geri Murray, Pam Myers, Ric Newton, Pauli Richards, Richard Tapper, and Dr. Molly Willett for giving me the jewels within friendship.

For my husband and family, my love and gratitude has always been, and will always be, very strong. Thank you so much Monica & Steven Bland, Lorie Leaf, Bruce Light, Alex & Charlotte Pick, for your precious gift of unconditional love.

Although it is out of the ordinary, I feel compelled to give credit where credit is due. My love and appreciation goes beyond words for "the Great Spirit" who lives within and around us all, without whom nothing, including this book, could be possible.

Table of Contents

APPENDIX

Part I

My Heart to Yours

You can't prevent the birds of
sadness from flying over your head,
but you can prevent them
from nesting in your hair.

Chinese Proverb

A New Journal

This is a new kind of journal. As you probably know, it isn't always easy breaking new ground. I imagine that one day journals such as this may be as common as high school yearbooks and will need no explanation. Since that day has yet to come, please allow me to introduce it.

This journal is a personal growth process. It gives you the opportunity to ponder your life and to embrace your death as part of it. It is a place where you can organize your thoughts and leave your affairs in order. When things are in order you usually feel better and putting something in writing can save a lot of confusion later.

This journal is a way to take responsibility for your life through the end. It is a way of offering nurturing and assistance to those whom you leave behind and a means of communicating with your loved ones after your death. It is a way for you to tell them your last wishes, pass on your wisdom, answer their questions, and share important events of your life with future generations. Received from someone you love, this journal can serve as a precious reminder of them. Left to those who love you, it becomes a very special gift.

An old saying,

"MAY HE REST IN PEACE"

I wonder what he did in his life to ensure that he would?

Edith

My grandmother Edith's health had been declining for years. I think everyone, including her, knew that she wouldn't be living much longer, yet no one talked about it. With her cancer spreading rapidly and numerous operations unable to help her, we began to take her death a little more seriously. My sister Lorie was the first to talk with Edith about how she felt about dying and the afterlife. That conversation broke the ice, and others of us in the family were then able to talk with her about her feelings.

Soon my grandmother had to spend more and more time in bed, and talking became difficult. Realizing that she could die any day, there was sudden urgency within all of us. *"WAIT, don't go yet; we want to know more about your history. How was it that you and Opa met? Tell me what your parents were like and how they made a living. Let us know your wishes. Do you want to be buried or cremated? Do you want a funeral? What should we do with all your things?"*

Filled with the emotions of losing someone you love, it can be extremely difficult to ask these and other questions, not only is it difficult, but it may not be a good time. When my grandmother was dying, she needed to rest and to have peace and quiet. Knowing there was so much unfinished business made her restless and upset. I kept asking myself over and over again, *"Why didn't we take care of all this a long time ago? What a mess to have to do it now while there is so much pain."*

Edith died slowly which gave us some time to prepare and have our questions answered. I was so grateful to have had some time with her to say good-bye. At the same time I felt well aware of all the people who aren't so lucky. Every day thousands of people lose someone they love with little or no warning. Thinking about that and seeing the confusion that surrounded my grandmother's death, formed a great part of my inspiration for putting together this book.

Thank you, Nanny, not only for giving me inspiration for this book, but especially for having the courage to die at home where all of us could experience with you your pain and fear, your surrendering and your letting go. Although it was often very challenging for us, we all learned a great deal. Each of us felt closer to you because of it. God bless you and may you rest in peace.

To conquer fear

is the beginning of wisdom.

Bertrand Russell

Let's Talk About What No One Talks About

Death is something which affects all of us, yet we rarely talk about it. I believe its lack of social expression is one reason why we fear it so much. I remember several years ago I was doubting my mental stability. I ultimately confided this feeling to a therapist. I was afraid he was going to agree with me, but instead he offered great relief by telling me that people tell him the same thing all the time. He said that most everyone at one time or another thinks they may go crazy. So I asked him why nobody talks about it, and he replied that they are too afraid.

Since then I have wanted to write a book entitled, *"1000 Things We All Think Of, But Nobody Talks About."* I feel inspired to write about these things because I feel they are often in direct relation to things that we fear. The more we expose our fears, the less power they will have to live within us. We can expose our fears by talking about them, listening to others talk about them, and by getting to know and accept them. I have found when I do this, I feel much lighter and happier. When I share with people the things that are hard to say, I feel much closer to them. In a recent letter discussing by father's estate, my brother wrote, "It's a very touchy subject, but isn't that what bonds people". Being vulnerable and taking risks may feel awkward but I believe it is essential for our personal

growth and well being. The key is to accept ourselves—our goodness as well as our "dark side"—and
know that, at our core, we are all the same. Our fears
are universal, and so is our longing for love.

Where there is love and acceptance there is the true
gift of life. The more love and the less fear we feel, the
more fully we experience life. By uncovering our fears
related to death we become more open to life. It may
be paradoxical, but I believe that it is true that by con-
fronting death we can begin to get out there and really
LIVE. It is important to pay some attention to death,
but what really matters is life. While you are alive,
release your fears and replace them with love whenever
you can. Remember what you were born for, your in-
tention and purpose, and do what you need to do in
order to feel complete by the end of your life.

How many times the rose has been
metaphorically abused
        I would not venture to guess.
To envision the growth of a human
    as the bud, bloom and decay
        of the rose may be far-fetched,
yet seems so appropriate.

Eric Clem

Eric

Eric was my lover and a very close friend. En route to his twenty-fourth birthday party, he died in a car accident. I am sure that never did he, nor did anyone that knew him, think that he would die so young and so suddenly.

After he died, his mother put together a little book of letters, poems, and journal entries that he had written. Contained in it he wrote:

"The other evening, while playing with a solid state, lightweight, miniature mind (a calculator), I discovered a dreadful fact: there are only 364 Friday nights left to my enjoyment until I am thirty. Is this reality? It's all so temporary. Everything is temporary."

I'm writing this on Eric's thirtieth birthday. Although he died six years ago, I still wish him a happy birthday, and I still miss him. With his death, I have learned the truth in what he was saying in his journal entry. Yes, everything is temporary. Life is a constant state of change, always moving. . .birth and death and birth. . . That everything will change and everything will die (just another change) is life's only guarantee.

I think that this lesson has taken awhile to really sink in. Just in this past year am I finally starting to "get on with my life." I am taking a good hard look at myself and saying, *"Okay, this is what I have got; now what am I going to do with it?"*

I am just beginning to live my life as if I weren't immortal. I don't claim to have the answers, but I have found that, by being more aware of my own mortality, I am able to be more fully "alive", and appreciate the days I am given. When I realize that I could die anyday I don't put things off. I try to keep my communications clear and updated. I ask people what I want to know about them and tell them what I want them to know about me. It has worked wonders for my relationships. Oh, how relationships thrive when people are not taken for granted!

Eric, I never took you for granted; only the time we had together. I don't understand much about these things called life and death. I only hope that whatever it is that the afterlife brings, you are enjoying the very best of it!

A civilization that denies death
ends by denying life.

Octavio Paz.

A Needed Journal

Dying is a fact of life yet we give it as little attention as possible. In our culture great preparations are made for important moments such as weddings, the arrivals of new babies, school graduations and anniversaries, but most of us do little or nothing to prepare for the one event that is inevitable.

The emphasis is on our bodies and how well we can cover up any sign of nearing the end of life. Elderly people are often isolated and ignored as if life's natural ripening process is unacceptable. In general we idolize good health and youth and deny the rest. This distorts our sense of natural existence and indeed the divine process. In blocking out pain and death, we close off a significant part of life. In so doing, we create fear and suffering for ourselves and others.

We need to bring the idea of death "out of the closet." We need to see that it too is an aspect of our lives deserving thoughtful attention. We likewise need to assume leadership in preparing for the personal and economic matters that arise from the event.

With inheritance laws controlling our personal giving, doctors and hospitals directing our health and our death, and the high cost of traditional funeral practices, it's time we make our own decisions about how we live and how we die.

The day we are born we
become a terminal case.

Garry Bland

Papa Bear

Two years ago in Alaska, my father, Garry, and I talked about his feeling about death. Above supressed tears he told me that the most important thing to him was that he would be remembered. This conversation certainly planted a seed for "Remembering Me".

Two weeks after the first edition of this book was off the press, my mother and I set out to distribute it. The book was well received and we were happy. Mom was great, so helpful and supportive. On the fourth morning of our trip I awoke and she was already on the phone. When she saw me she hung up abruptly. As she sat me down she gently said, "Dad has had a heart attack". A dam broke inside of me. By her voice and actions I knew it was bad. Finally, I drummed up the courage to ask how bad. She said he was in a coma and they didn't expect him to come out of it. My guts twisted and I cried what mom called "hysterically".

Soon my sister joined us and we all flew to Los Angeles. My sister and mother were "strong", while I was a barely functioning black cloud. In a daze, I stumbled into my father's hospital room. I took his hand and he squeezed mine. My sister, Lorie, thanked him for waiting for us. We were all so glad that he was still alive.

In the following days I stayed with him from morning till night. There was nowhere else I wanted to be. During this time I talked to him and stroked his hair.

I cried and I sat in silence. I filled out his copy of "Remembering Me" and I began writing in mine. I created an altar for him of pictures, flowers, a teddy bear I had given him and another one I had bought at the hospital gift shop because it wore a tie which read "Number One Dad". I played his favorite music as well as music which comforted me. One evening Lorie and I sang to him. Never have I heard our voices so beautiful. Both of us ventured to raise his eyelids. Some doubt that people in a coma can see or hear, but we knew he could. He was aware of our presence and we were all very grateful to be together.

Knowing he was not going to recover, our family circled around him to say good-bye. Because it rarely happened, it had meant so much to me to see our family all together. Painfully, I accepted that this was the last time. We had decided to shut off his life support machines. Luckily, we all knew that Dad would not have wanted to be kept alive by heroic measures. This helped us tremendously to make the most difficult decision of our lives. It was time to release him and let him go.

The morning we came to say our final good-bye, they had moved my father to another room. Since we were going to turn off his life support, there was no reason to keep him in intensive care. Now he had a roommate, a senile man in rage. During my father's final hours we had to listen to the poor fellow yell about his wife and his bed pan. Here I learned the need for hospitals to have an "Alternative Dying Room" where families could have peace and privacy when they need it most. Still, we concentrated on Dad. I sensed "angels" in the room and as my father died I felt his spirit leaving his body. With all my heart I wished him a good journey. In between the tears, there was peace. I waited for awhile in the stillness of the room. I wanted to be with my thoughts and pray for my father, but shortly after his death, the nurse came in and said, "Will you be much longer?" Needless to say, I decided to take my feelings elsewhere.

After leaving the hospital I was aware of a hole inside of me from head to toe. In the weeks that followed I gave myself time to recover. Then the hole disappeared. I had filled it with myself. Profoundly I experienced the maturing process. My healing had gently taken place as I let my thoughts and emotions run their natural course.

Papa Bear, our love is beyond death as true love does not die. Over and over again, I wish to thank you for your friendship, for giving me "Oscar," and for being the best father you could be. This poem is for you and for anyone who has lost someone as precious as you are to me.

DEATH'S INTERNAL SPLIT

Rational mind knew it would happen,
   the rest of me can not grasp it.
Reasoning mind says he had a long life,
   while I scream, "No! It wasn't long enough".
Common sense told me it could be anytime,
   but I didn't think it would be now.
Philosophical self remarks on the timing and that "It was
   meant to be".
Angrily I demand to know why I wasn't warned.
Spiritual self sees death's illusion and whispers "Spirit lives
   forever", while my body longs to hold him.
Faith gently and quietly accepts his death,
   as denial is a crying wild horse.
Integration occurs as I allow each voice to be heard,
   and recognized as loving my father.

Nothing is sweeter than love,
nothing stronger, nothing loftier,
nothing grander, nothing
pleasanter, nothing fuller,
nothing better in heaven or earth.

Henri Matisse

With Love

If questions arise about how to give this book to someone close, reflect on the love the two of you share. When we communicate with love, all actions are graciously accepted. Love makes us naturally sensitive and tactful. Forget about what someone may think and just remember your compassion.

Giving this book to someone does not mean you advocate their death. Actually, you are encouraging their life fully, from beginning to end. You're affirming two of life's most wonderous aspects; caring and self expression. The book can provide an impetus to touching a loved one in a very deep way. Truly loving another is supporting them through whatever they're experiencing. The quality of your shared love will ideally remain constant when things are both comfortable and when they are difficult, when someone is healthy and when they are dying.

Our culture seems to be obsessed with "the bright side". When asked how we are doing we are expected to answer, "Fine" or "Couldn't be better". There doesn't seem to be room for anything else. We are often not totally open to one another because of our discomfort with the full experience of life within ourselves. To love another we must be willing to embrace every part of ourselves, including our fears. As we discover the joy in self acceptance we become a beacon of hope for others. This self love and acceptance will also nourish us in the most challenging of life's transitions. As we continue growing, an open heart and mind are our greatest allies and the best we have to offer others.

Part II

Your Heart to Theirs

*The unexamined life
is not worth living.*

Plato

Suggestions For Using This Book

The following guidelines will assist you in filling your book. You certainly are not limited to these suggestions and should feel free to add your own questions and answers. Some sections may not be appropriate for you, and you may want to skip them altogether. You may feel an area was missed and want to add a section. Just be sure to include anything that you find meaningful.

As the years go by, you will probably find yourself revising and adding to the book; therefore, I suggest that you date all entries. There are several extra pages in the back of the last section should you need more room. You may want to keep some pages in a safe or separate place; some you may later decide to delete. If you take out things that I have written, I promise not to be offended.

Take this journal as seriously or as lightly as you choose. Spend as much or as little time with it as you like. As the old saying goes, *"You'll get out of it what you put into it."* Preparing this journal certainly has the potential to be an enlightening experience for you and a treasure for all those who wish to remember you. Once again, this is *YOUR* journal. Have fun; enjoy it!

Pictures

Include one or several pictures of yourself. Maybe ones of various ages and/or expressions. You may want to add pictures which would hold no particular meaning to others, yet are special to you. You may want to put captions underneath them. If you feel inspired, draw or paint a picture. You might even use a picture from a magazine, or several of them, and create a collage. Place pictures in chronological order or at random. Tell a story with your pictures, remembering that, *"a picture is worth a thousand words."*

My Favorite Things

What are your interests and hobbies? What is your favorite music? Which seasons are special to you? Do you have a collection of prized possessions? What are your favorite foods, places to visit, articles of clothing? Do you like animals? Which ones? Do you have a favorite poem or joke? Mention some books and/or films you found especially enjoyable. If you feel like it, talk about your favorite holidays. How do you spend your free time? What really gets you feeling good?

Celebrating

Take time to sit back and appreciate the many wonderful aspects of yourself. Talk about your talents and abilities (don't be modest). What are the things people praise you for. What is it about yourself you are proud of? Share your strengths as well as your weaknesses. Acknowledge every part of yourself. Describe yourself to someone who longs to know you better. Celebrate yourself, just the way you are!

Looking Back

This is the time to reminisce. Go back to the beginning; look back through the years. What do you see? How was it? Give a factual outline of your life. Identify turning points in your life. Talk about the people who were the most influential at various stages of your development. Describe jobs that you have held and organizations with which you were affiliated. Recall whatever was most meaningful to you. Note the good times along with the difficult ones. Do an autobiography as simple or as detailed as you choose. However you choose to write it, remember to give yourself a lot of credit for making it through all that you have!

Looking Ahead

Think about the future. If you were to live for many more years, what would you like to do? If you have dreams, write about them. Don't worry about how idealistic they may seem. If you have unlimited resources, where would you go and what would you do? What goals do you have and what plans do you have to achieve them? Describe your life ten or twenty years from now. What do you really hope for in the future?

My Living Will

A living will allows you to instruct your doctor not to use artificial methods to extend the natural process of dying. It is a way for you to take responsibility for the ultimate decision about your life and death. If you wish to have a living will I have included one in this section. I have also included a blank page so that you can write your feelings on this subject. Please understand that "Living Wills" are not honored in all states and that doctors are not always obligated to accept them. However, if you desire to have a living will then go ahead and write one because it will be a clear statement of your wishes. In California there is a document called a *Durable Power of Attorney for Health Care,* which allows you to select someone to make health care decisions for you if you become unable to make them yourself. You can get this document from your doctor or the California Medical Association. Your local "Home Hospice" can inform you of the current laws in your state as well as answer any questions you may have on the subject.

If you decide to use the living will that I have included, it should be witnessed by two people who are not related to you by blood or marriage. They should not be mentioned in your will and not be your future care providers. Discuss your intentions with those closest to you now. Glance over your living will once a year; redate it and initial the new date to make it clear that you endorse the contents of the will as it presently reads.

What To Do With My Body

There are three methods of disposition. These are (1) earth burial or vault entombment, (2) cremation and Calcination® (similar to cremation, but does not use an open flame or chemicals), and (3) donation of body or organs. If you want to be buried, specify where. When making arrangements visit several funeral homes. Ask for an itemized price list. Find out if they will honor your personal preferences. Select one based on its service, reputation and cost. You can find out about laws governing burial through your local Board of Health or County Coroner. If you wish to be cremated, express that desire. Be sure to let your family know what you would like done with your ashes. To donate your body or particular organs you will need to make arrangements with your chosen hospital, research or educational institute. Sign a Uniform Donor Card and carry it with you. Funeral plans are required in almost every case of organ donation. When a whole body is donated, a memorial service may still be held.

Many people are eligible for help with funeral expenses. Some possibilities include insurance, trade unions, fraternal organizations, social security and veterans administration. Although your survivors must apply, you can gather information and/or set up a Funeral Trust Account which will help them later. You may also want to check with a non-profit Memorial Society that assists members in making pre-arrangements for simple, economical funerals. If you decide to join one of the numerous Memorial Societies or have made any pre-arrangements for your burial, let your famliy know that you have done so.

Burial Ceremonies

This is another way of celebrating yourself. You can help to create your own ceremony! My grandmother requested that her ceremony be simple and brief and that Beethoven be played in the background. Do you have requests concerning music or the place where the funeral is to be held? Do you have a favorite poem or prayer you would like read? Do you have a favorite flower? Do you have a special minister, priest, rabbi or friend who you would like to have speak? You may invite those who wish to speak or participate to do so. It may be your desire not to have any ceremony at all.

Express how you feel and let your wishes be known. Remember that it is certainly all right to ask for what you want. Your loved ones will want to oblige your wishes; it makes them feel good.

Consider your loved ones and what may please them. It is a meaningful time for the living as it gives them an opportunity to express their grief, their faith, and offer support to one another. The funeral can also aid survivors in accepting the reality of death. Design a funeral that will reflect your life and will also be understood by those who will attend. This is a time when all the love which people feel for you comes out. It is a very special time.

What To Do With My Possessions — My Will

This is your opportunity to express how you would like your material possessions distributed after your death. Who do you want to administer the distribution of your things (called a personal representative or an executor)? What exactly would you like to leave and to whom? If your children are minors, who shall have custody of them?

These are important questions to answer when you write your will. You can write your will yourself or see a lawyer for help. If your estate is large, it is a good idea to have a lawyer help you prepare your will to avoid potential legal pitfalls and obtain advantageous estate and inheritance tax advice. If you wish to write your own will, it is certainly legal to do so. I recommend the book, "*How to Write Your Own Will*" by John C. Howell (1985, Liberty Publishing Co., 50 Scott Adam Rd., Cockeysville, MD 21030, $9.95). Estate planning can save a lot of money on taxes. Two publications available at your local IRS office may be helpful: #559, *Tax Information for Survivors, Executors and Administrators,* and #448, *A Guide to Federal Estate and Gift Taxation.* If your will is located somewhere outside of this book give its location and the name of the executor you have chosen. Most importantly, allow yourself to enjoy this part of your preparations. This is your chance to play Santa Claus like never before!

Wisdom I Wish to Pass On

This may be anything you have learned as you have gone through the years. What was the best advice you received? What values would you want to pass on to future generations? If you were to preach a sermon, what would you talk about? If you had enough power, how would you change the world? If you could hang a motto or saying in every home, what would it be? If you were to produce a book or a film, what would it be about? What wise things did you learn from your mother and father? What has your own life taught you? What words of wisdom do you have for those you will leave behind? Include your own thoughts as well as what you have gained from others. Share what has helped and inspired you along the way.

Afterlife

Use these pages to write your beliefs about the afterlife. Do you believe you have a soul that leaves your body when you die? If so, what do you believe happens next? What will it be like? Do you believe in reincarnation? If you haven't done so already, share whatever religious beliefs you have. If you feel so inclined, include a prayer for yourself. If you are agnostic, express those feelings. Allow your heart to guide you to the knowledge you have within about life after death, for all answers are inside of you!

Remember, I Love You

Personally speaking, this is my favorite part of the book. I admit to being a "sentimental fool" and thus, the idea of lots of people writing "remember, I love you" to lots of other people really excites me. Beyond that, this is my favorite part because I feel so strongly about telling people how much you care for them. Living with all the troubles we have both inside and out, receiving compassion from others, can really help to balance things out. Most of us rarely say to a friend, "I really like you." We compliment them, yet generally feel awkward expressing our feelings directly. I deeply encourage you to express your love any way you can, while you are alive. These pages are for the things you never said or just want to say again in writing. Tell your relatives and friends how much you love and appreciate them. Tell them things they would enjoy hearing. Above anything else in this book, they will cherish these pages as long as they live.

Notes

The purpose of this section is for you to include any further information that may help your family upon your death. It is a general section where you can incorporate anything you like. There are several outlines in this section. One outline is a list of people you would like notified when you "pass on". Do you have a special message for any of these people? Is there something you can suggest for your family and friends to think about that will ease their emotions? Would you like to draw a "family tree" or add information about relatives that have gone before you. You can place copies of your birth certificate, veterans' discharge papers and other important documents with this book or you can use this section to inform your family where they are located. There are extra pages in this section in case you didn't have enough room in the previous sections. Maybe here you will want to create a section. Add whatever may be missing until the book feels complete and you feel content.

Remembering Me

written by_______________________________

Pictures

My Favorite Things

Celebrating

Looking Back

Looking Ahead

My Living Will

To My Family, My Physician, My Lawyer and All Others Whom It May Concern

Death is as much a reality as birth, growth, maturity and old age—it is one certainty of life. If the time comes when I can no longer take part in decisions for my own future, let this statement stand as an expression of my wishes and directions, while I am of sound mind.

If at such a time the situation should arise in which there is no reasonable expection of my recovery from extreme physical or mental disability, I direct that I be allowed to die and not be kept alive by medications, artificial means or "heroic measures". I do, however, ask that medication be mercifully administered to me to alleviate suffering even though this may shorten my remaining life.

This statement is made after careful consideration and is in accordance with my strong convictions and beliefs. I want the wishes and directions here expressed carried out to the extent permitted by law. Insofar as they are not legally enforceable, I hope that those to whom this Will is addressed will regard themselves as morally bound by these provisions.

Signed _______________________

Date _______________________

Witness _______________________

Witness _______________________

Copies of this request have been given to _______________

____

____

____

What To Do With
My Body

Burial Ceremonies

What To Do With My Possessions— My Will

Wisdom I Wish to Pass On

Afterlife

Remember, I love You

Notes

STATISTICAL RECORD

Full Name ____

Address _____________________ (city) _________________________

(county) ______________ (state) ____________ (zip) ____________

I have resided in this state since ________________________

Prior residence in _________________ for ________ years.

Birthdate ___________________ Birthplace ____________________

(If foreign born) I entered U.S.A. __________________ .Citizen

of what country or date of U.S. naturalization ___________ .

Usual Occupation ______________________________________ .

Social Security Number _______________________________ .

Marital Status ____________ Spouse's Name ______________

Spouse's Maiden Name, Birthdate and Birthplace _______

____ .

Date and Place of Marriage _______________________________ .

Father's Full Name ____ .

Father's Birthplace _______________________________________ .

Mother's Full Name (maiden) ______________________________ .

Mother's Birthplace _______________________________________ .

Name and Address of Next of Kin __________________________

____

PERSONAL INVENTORY

Employer ____

Company Benefits _______________________________________

If copies of my birth certificate and Veteran's discharge papers
are not located with this book, you will find them

____

INSURANCE

Life: _____________________ Policy No. ___________

Health & Accident: _________ Policy No. ___________

Automobile: _______________ Policy No. ___________

Other:____________________ Policy No. ___________

BANKING PAPERS

Kind of Account   Bank Name/Address   Account Number

_____________   _______________   ____________

_____________   _______________   ____________

_____________   _______________   ____________

Safety Deposit Box Number ______________________________

Bank Name/Address _____________________________________

Location of Key _______________________________________

AUTOMOBILES (Make, Model, Year, License Number)

____

____

REAL ESTATE PAPERS (Location of Deeds)

____

____

PERSONAL ITEMS OF VALUE

____

____

____

____

RELATIVES AND FRIENDS TO NOTIFY

Name________________________   Phone____________________

Address____

Special Messages ____

____

____

____

Name____ Phone

Address____

Special Messages ____

____

____

Name________________________   Phone____________________

Address____

Special Messages ____

____

____

____

Name____ Phone

Address____

Special Messages ____

____

____

Name________________________   Phone____________________

Address____

Special Messages ____

____

____

Name_______________________   Phone___________________

Address ____

Special Messages ____

____

____

____

Name____ Phone

Address ____

Special Messages ____

____

____

Name_______________________   Phone___________________

Address ____

Special Messages ____

____

____

____

Name____ Phone

Address ____

Special Messages ____

____

____

Name_______________________   Phone___________________

Address ____

Special Messages ____

____

____

____

Name_____________________ Phone_____________________
Address____

Name_____________________ Phone_____________________
Address____

Name_____________________ Phone_____________________
Address____

Name_____________________ Phone_____________________
Address____

Name_____________________ Phone_____________________
Address____

Name_____________________ Phone_____________________
Address____

Name_____________________ Phone_____________________
Address____

Name_____________________ Phone_____________________
Address____

Name_____________________ Phone_____________________
Address____

Name_____________________ Phone_____________________
Address____

Name_____________________ Phone_____________________
Address____

Name_____________________ Phone_____________________
Address____

Name_____________________ Phone_____________________
Address____

PEOPLE WHO CAN HELP WITH MY AFFAIRS

Attorney _______________________________________

Banker ____

Insurance Agent ________________________________

Doctor ____

Clergy ____

Business Associates ____________________________

____

Broker ____

Accountant _____________________________________

Others ____

____

____

____

____

____

____

MILITARY SERVICE

Name of War ____________________________________

Rank________________Serial Number________________

Date Enlisted ________Date Discharged __________

Location of Discharge Papers_____________________

Appendix

What To Do when Someone Dies

When someone close to you dies—first of all take care of yourself. Get the rest and nurturing that you need. Do not suppress your emotions or they will build up inside of you. Feel the love as well as the pain, fear and anger. Accept yourself for feeling whatever you do. Allow others to help and support you and also take the alone time you need. Take the time for a private ceremony. If you feel like it, talk to the person who has just died. Possibly you will sense their response. Bodies die, but love never does. Acknowledge the feelings you have for the person and give thanks for the time you had together. When you are ready, release and let them go. Wish them a smooth journey.

Listed below are some of the things you will need to do. This check list comes from *"A Manual Of Death Education and Simple Burial"* by Ernest Morgan and is available through Celo Press and most memorial societies. Remember to take care of yourself first and allow others to help you.

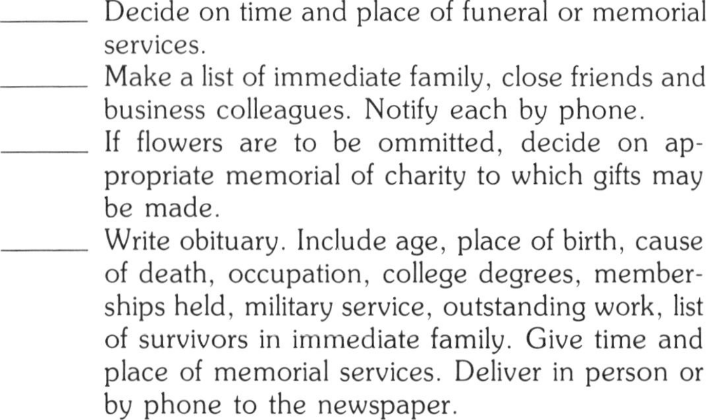

________ Decide on time and place of funeral or memorial services.

________ Make a list of immediate family, close friends and business colleagues. Notify each by phone.

________ If flowers are to be ommitted, decide on appropriate memorial of charity to which gifts may be made.

________ Write obituary. Include age, place of birth, cause of death, occupation, college degrees, memberships held, military service, outstanding work, list of survivors in immediate family. Give time and place of memorial services. Deliver in person or by phone to the newspaper.

A

_______ Notify insurance companies, including automobile insurance for immediate cancellation and refund of premium.

_______ Arrange for members of the family or close friends to take turns answering door or phone, keeping careful record of calls.

_______ Arrange appropriate child care.

_______ Coordinate the supplying of food for the next days.

_______ Consider special needs of the household, such as cleaning which might be done by freinds.

_______ Arrange hospitality for visiting relatives and friends.

_______ Select pall bearers and notify. (Avoid men with heart or back difficulties, or make them honorary pall bearers.)

_______ Notify lawyer and personal representative.

_______ Plan for disposition of flowers after funeral (give to a hospital or rest home?).

_______ Prepare list of persons living at a distance to be notified by letter or printed notice, and decide which to send to each.

_______ Prepare the message for printed notice if one is wanted.

_______ Prepare list of people to receive acknowledgements. (May be written notes, printed acknowledgements, or some of each.)

_______ Check carefully all life and casuality insurance policies and death benefits including Social Security, credit union, trade union, fraternal, military, etc. Check also on income for survivors from these sources.

_______ Check promptly on all debts, mortgages, and installment payments. Some may carry life insurance clauses that will cancel the debt. If there is a delay in meeting payments, consult with creditors and ask for more time before the payments are due.

_______ If deceased was living alone, notify utilities and landlord and tell post office where to send mail. Take precautions against thieves.

One thing at a time . . .

A World of Caring

This book is just a beginning toward exploring the growing field of death and dying. Now that you have begun to examine this area of your life you may feel inspired to research it further. If so, I support you in doing so and offer the following helpful resources.

Books

Anatomy of an Illness as Perceived by the Patient: Reflections on Healing and Regenerations by Norman Cousins
How Can I Help? Stories and Reflections on Service by Ram Dass and Paul Gorman.
Coming Home, A guide to Home Care for the Terminally Ill by Deborah Duda
Love is Letting Go of Fear by Gerald Jampolsky
Death, the Final Stage of Growth - Questions and Answers on Death and Dying - To Live Until We Say Goodbye by Elisabeth Kubler-Ross
Meetings at the Edge - Who Dies? by Steven Levine
Life After Life by Raymond Moody M.D.
A Manual Of Death Education and Simple Burial by Ernest Morgan
Living Beyond Fear by Jeanne Segal, Ph. D.
A Practical Guide to Death and Dying, How to Conquer Your Fear and Anxiety Through a Program of personal Action by John White

Organizations

Hospice may be the first people you will want to contact as they will be able to answer many of your questions and give you local references. As there are now over 1,200 hospices in the U.S. you should find a listing in your phone

B

book. If you have trouble locating their number you can contact the national headquarters.

National Hospice Organization
1901 No. Ft. Myer Drive
Arlington, VA 22209
(703) 243-5900

Shanti Nilaya is a center founded by Elisabeth Kubler-Ross. They offer retreats regularly for dying patients, their families and professionals in the field.

Shanti Nilaya
Star Route A-Box 28
Headwaters, VA 24442

Society of the Right to Die works for the individual's right to die with dignity. They will send you Living Will Declarations and other appropriate documents authorized by right-to-die laws.

Society for the Right to Die
250 W. 57th Street
New York, New York 10107
(212) 246-6973

Funeral and Memorial Societies are listed in the white pages of your phone book. If you need assistance you can contact the Continental Association in Washington, D.C.

The Continental Association of Funeral & Memorial Societies
2001 S Street, N.W., Suite 530
Washington, DC 20009

Friends

Friends are often our greatest resource for information and support. Ask your friends what books they recommend. When someone close to them died, what did they find helpful? Share your ideas with each other. Remember, friends can be good medicine!

Danielle

Photo by Donn Brannon

Looking Back

My life has been a mixture of laughter and love, doubt and pain, opening and closing. Its sum total: quiet tears of joy.

Life has brought me a treasure of experience. I have taught developmentally disabled adults and worked in social services with all ages. My work with health retreats has satisfied my desire to see people (including myself) take time out for themselves. I have always loved sports, travelling, and making new friends. Looking back, it has been a very good life indeed!

Looking Ahead

My husband and I are currently restoring Mt. Shasta's (in northern California) oldest motor court. We are calling it "The Light Blew Inn". We hope to create a comfortable "Home away from home" for travelers as well as a place for workshops and retreats. I would also like to journey across the country, sharing the concept of this book with social service organizations.

While I am alive I want to live life to the fullest. I want to know the world within myself as well as the one around me. Above all, I want to continue to increase my capability to give and receive love.

C

If you would like additional copies of **Remembering Me** by Danielle Light, please fill out the form below and send it with your check or money order and any comments you have to:

Mt. Shasta Publications
P.O. Box 436
Mt. Shasta, CA 96067

Please send ____ copies of **Remembering Me** @ *$7.95 ea.*

Amount $________________

In Calif. add 6% tax $________________
Postage & Handling $________________*(.75ᶜ per book*
**Total Enclosed* $________________ *$2.00 maximum)*

Ship to: ____
Address: ____
City:________________________ State:________ Zip:________

* For orders of 6 or more books, deduct 15% from the total.

D

To every thing there is a season, and
a time to every purpose under heaven:

A time to be born, and a time to
die; a time to plant, and a time to
pluck up that which is planted;

A time to kill, and a time to heal;
a time to break down and a time
to build up;

A time to weep, and a time to
laugh; a time to mourn, and a time to
dance;

A time to cast away stones, and a time
to gather stones together; a time to
embrace, and a time to refrain from
embracing;

A time to get, and a time to lose;
a time to keep, and a time to cast away;

A time to rend, and a time to sew; a
time to keep silence, and a time to speak;

A time to love, and a time to hate;
a time of war, and a time of peace.

Ecclesiastes
King James Version
Chapter 3